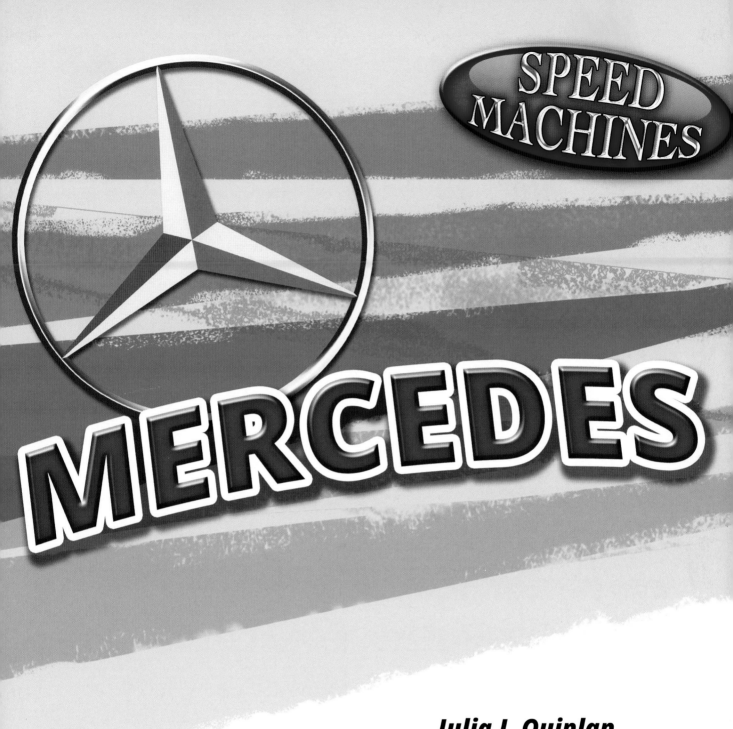

SPEED MACHINES

MERCEDES

Julia J. Quinlan

PowerKiDS
press™

New York

Published in 2014 by The Rosen Publishing Group, Inc.
29 East 21st Street, New York, NY 10010

First Edition

Editor: Jennifer Way
Book Design: Greg Tucker
Book Layout: Kate Vlachos

Photo Credits: Cover © iStockphoto.com/Marin Tomas; pp. 4–5, 20 DDCoral/Shutterstock.com; p. 6 Hulton Archive/Getty Images; p. 7 Car Culture/Getty Images; p. 8 Palo_ok/Shutterstock.com; p. 9 Mondadori/Getty Images; p. 10 Gustavo Fadel/Shutterstock.com; p. 11 Philip Lange/Shutterstock.com; p. 12 Thomas Kienzle/AFP/Getty Images; p. 13 Josep Lago/AFP/Getty Images; pp. 14–15 David Acosta Allely/Shutterstock.com; pp. 16–17, 18, 19 Dariusz Majgier/Shutterstock.com; p. 21 from http://en.wikipedia.org/wiki/File:2010_Mercedes-Benz_E350_--_NHTSA.jpg; pp. 22–23 © Transtock/SuperStock; pp. 24, 27 dutourdumonde/Shutterstock.com; p. 25 Stefan Ataman/Shutterstock.com; p. 26 Gyuszko-Photo/Shutterstock.com; pp. 28–29 Robin Marchant/Getty Images Entertainment/Getty Images.

Library of Congress Cataloging-in-Publication Data

Quinlan, Julia J.
 Mercedes / by Julia J. Quinlan. — First edition.
     pages cm. — (Speed machines)
 Includes index.
 ISBN 978-1-4777-0809-5 (library binding) — ISBN 978-1-4777-0990-0 (paperback) —
 ISBN 978-1-4777-0991-7 (6-pack)
 1. Mercedes automobile—Juvenile literature. I. Title.
 TL215.M4Q85 2014
 629.222—dc23
                              2013000201

Manufactured in the United States of America

CPSIA Compliance Information: Batch #S13PK8: For Further Information contact Rosen Publishing, New York, New York at 1-800-237-9932

Contents

German Quality

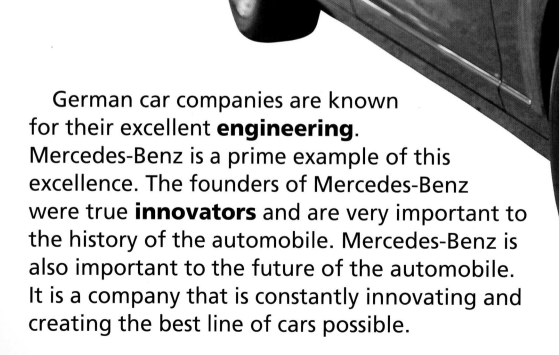

Here is a 2012 S 500. S-Class cars are known for being Mercedes' most luxurious models.

German car companies are known for their excellent **engineering**. Mercedes-Benz is a prime example of this excellence. The founders of Mercedes-Benz were true **innovators** and are very important to the history of the automobile. Mercedes-Benz is also important to the future of the automobile. It is a company that is constantly innovating and creating the best line of cars possible.

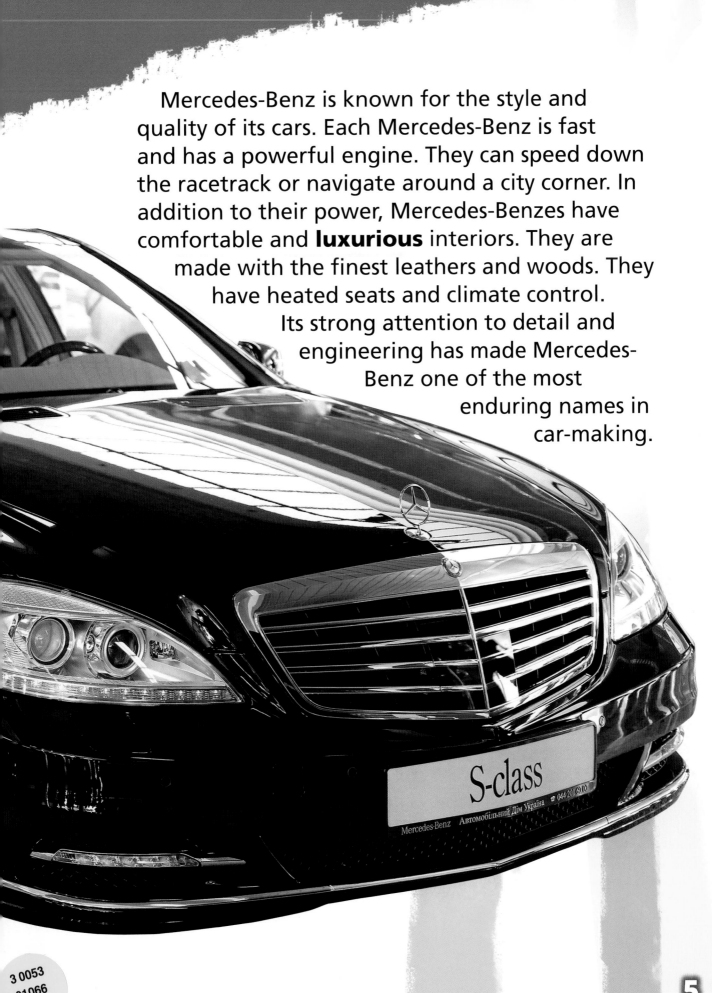

Mercedes-Benz is known for the style and quality of its cars. Each Mercedes-Benz is fast and has a powerful engine. They can speed down the racetrack or navigate around a city corner. In addition to their power, Mercedes-Benzes have comfortable and **luxurious** interiors. They are made with the finest leathers and woods. They have heated seats and climate control. Its strong attention to detail and engineering has made Mercedes-Benz one of the most enduring names in car-making.

Early Innovators

The founders of the two companies that joined together to make Mercedes-Benz were responsible for some of the most important innovations in car-making. In fact, one of these founders was involved in the invention of the automobile itself! Karl Benz founded a company called Benz & Cie. in 1883 and **patented** the first car in 1886. It was a three-wheeled "motorwagen." It had two wheels in the back and one wheel in the front.

Karl Benz

Here is the three-wheeled "motorwagen" that Benz patented in 1886.

Between the front and back wheels was a bench for the driver and a passenger. It had a rear-mounted one-cylinder engine and a top speed of 10 miles per hour (16 km/h).

One of Benz's **competitors** was Daimler-Motoren-Gesellschaft, or DMG. This company was founded in 1890 by Gottlieb Daimler and Wilhelm Maybach. DMG was also responsible for important innovations. In 1894, it built an engine it called the Phoenix. This groundbreaking four-cylinder engine allowed cars to reach 25 miles per hour (40 km/h).

Two Companies Become One

Benz & Cie. and DMG were competitors during the late 1800s and early 1900s. After **World War I**, however, the European **economy** was bad. It was hard for luxury companies like them to stay in business. In 1926, DMG and Benz & Cie. joined together to stay in business. The new company was called Daimler-Benz AG. Later, the name was changed to Mercedes-Benz.

The "Mercedes" in the name comes from Emil Jellinek, a wealthy businessman. In 1901, he **commissioned** a DMG car and had it named for his daughter, Mercedes.

The Mercedes-Benz logo

Here is Karl Benz (third from right) posing with his family and one of his early cars.

The Mercedes-Benz logo is a combination of the two original companies' logos. The three-pointed star was trademarked by DMG in 1909. Benz & Cie. began using a laurel as their symbol in 1903. The star was put inside the laurel to create the original Mercedes-Benz logo. That logo evolved into today's three-pointed star within a circle.

Many Mercedes

Today, Mercedes-Benz has 12 different car series. Each series features several different models. Each series of cars covers a different price range. Mercedes-Benz makes both very expensive, **exclusive** models and more affordable models. That means that Mercedes-Benz appeals to a wide range of people. There is the C-Class at the lower end, with models starting at $35,000. Then there is the SLS-Class, with models starting at $200,000!

The W212 E-Class coupe, shown here, has been in production since 2009.

The M-Class is a Mercedes line of SUVs. Mercedes has had three generations of this line of SUVs since 1997.

Mercedes-Benz makes many different types of cars. It makes **sedans**, which have four doors. It makes coupes, which have two doors. It also makes convertibles, SUVs, and station wagons. Mercedes-Benz has several models that are **hybrids**. Hybrid cars use both gasoline and electricity to run. They use less gasoline and produce fewer **pollutants**. Hybrid cars are better for the environment and save owners money on gas.

Early Racers

Mercedes-Benz has a long racing history. One of Karl Benz's cars raced in the very first automobile race, in 1894! It was held in Paris. Unfortunately, Benz's car finished in 14th place. Mercedes-Benz has come a long way since that first race and its car have taken part in many international races. In the 1920s and 1930s, Mercedes-Benz cars raced in Grand Prix races around Europe.

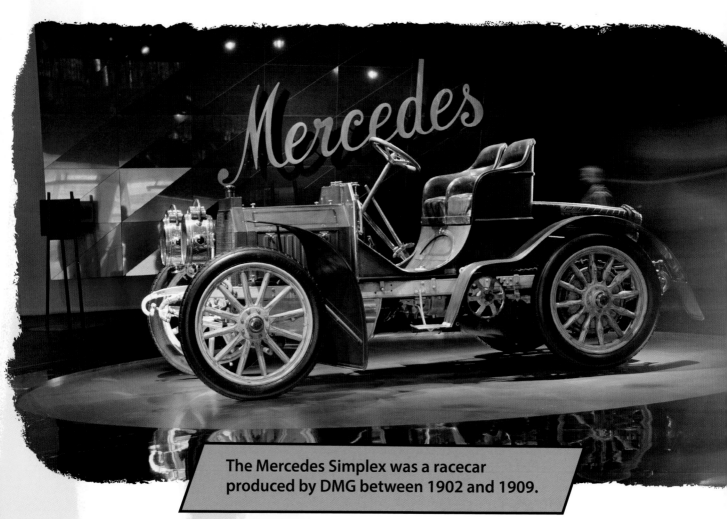

The Mercedes Simplex was a racecar produced by DMG between 1902 and 1909.

Nico Rosberg (left) and Michael Schumacher (right) were members of the 2012 Mercedes AMG Petronas F1 racing team.

Mercedes-Benz raced in Formula One in 1954 and 1955. After a terrible accident in another competition, in 1955, Mercedes-Benz withdrew from racing altogether. The accident happened at the 24 Hours of Le Mans in France. In 1994, Mercedes-Benz returned to Formula One as an engine supplier. This means that it built engines for various race teams. The current Mercedes-Benz Formula One team started in 2010. It is called Mercedes AMG Petronas. The engines for the Mercedes-Benz Formula One cars are built in England.

Racecars

Mercedes-Benz has been making racecars since its beginnings. Most luxury sports car makers make racecars. It is a way to show people how fast and powerful they can make their cars. Racecars are different from sports cars. They are made only for speed and control, not for style, comfort, or practical uses. In fact, it is illegal to drive a racecar on a road that is not a racetrack. Racecars are lower to the ground and more **aerodynamic** than sports cars.

The 2012 Mercedes-Benz racecar is the F1 W03. It looks more like a spaceship than a car. The body is very narrow and shaped to be as aerodynamic as possible. It has a 2.4-liter V8 engine.

The Mercedes F1 W03, shown here, was built for the 2012 Formula One season.

Ponton

The Mercedes Ponton was a car series made from 1953 until 1962. The Ponton is important to Mercedes-Benz's history because it was its first new model produced after **World War II**. Most of the company's factories were destroyed during the war. By 1953, the company was able to start making cars again, and the European economy was beginning to recover. With a better economy, more people could buy new cars.

There were many different versions of the Ponton. Some had four-cylinder engines, others had six-cylinder engines. There were hardtops and convertibles. One of the first Pontons was the W120 180. It came out in 1953. It was a four-door sedan with accentuated headlights. It was not a very fast model. Its top speed was only 78 mph (126 km/h), and it took 31 seconds to go from 0 to 60 miles per hour (0–97 km/h).

1953 Ponton 180

Engine size	1.8 liters
Number of cylinders	4
Transmission	Manual
Gearbox	4 speeds
0–60 mph (0–97 km/h)	31 seconds
Top speed	78 mph (126 km/h)

The 1959 W121 190D, shown here, was part of Mercedes' Ponton series.

W114 & W115

The W114 and W115 began production in 1968. They were different versions of the same car. The W114 had a six-cylinder engine, while the W115 had a four-cylinder engine. These models are often called "Strich Acht." "Strich Acht" is German for "slash eight." These cars had ID plates with a "/8" on them to show the year they went into production, 1968.

Mercedes W114 and W115 models were in production until 1976.

1968 Strich Acht

Engine size	2.3 liters
Number of cylinders	5
Transmission	Manual
Gearbox	4 speeds
0–60 mph (0–97 km/h)	4.9 seconds
Top speed	99 mph (159 km/h)

The W114 and W115 models replaced the W110 model, shown here.

The W114 was the first post–World War II model to have a completely new **chassis** design. Paul Bracq designed the W114 and W115. Bracq is a car designer who designed many cars for Mercedes-Benz.

Mercedes-Benz introduced new variations of the W114 and W115 during their production years, including a coupe version. Coupes have two doors instead of four. The coupe version had a six-cylinder engine.

E-Class

The Mercedes-Benz E-Class has been around for a long time. The 1953 W120 Ponton was actually the first E-Class. The modern E-Class began production in 2009 and is still being made. It is called the W212. The W212 was based on the W124, which was produced in the 1980s.

The E-Class line includes a station wagon, a coupe, and a convertible. The convertible version is shown here.

2010 E-Class Sedan

Engine size	3.5 liters (V6) or 5.5 liters (V8)
Number of cylinders	6 or 8
Transmission	Automatic
Gearbox	7 speeds
0–60 mph (0–97 km/h)	4.9 seconds
Top speed	155 mph (249 km/h)

This is an E-Class sedan.

The E-Class is Mercedes' mid-priced line of cars. They are more expensive than C-Class cars, but less expensive than S-Class cars. The E-Class is available in several different styles of car. There are E-Class sedans, coupes, cabriolets, and station wagons. The cabriolet is a convertible. The station wagon is much longer than the sedan. It has lots of space in the back for luggage or groceries.

GL-Class

The Mercedes-Benz GL-Class is a series of SUVs that began production in 2007. The GL-Class is still in production today. The GL-Class currently has three different versions. They are the GL350 BlueTEC, the GL450 4Matic, and the GL550 4Matic. The GL550 4Matic is the most expensive at around $90,000.

The GL-Class SUVs are extremely roomy and comfortable inside. They have luxurious features like heated seats. They also have a third row of seats that can fold up and down on their own! There is the option to put in massaging leather seats instead of standard seats. The GL-Class is made to be extremely comfortable, but also powerful. The body of the car was designed to be aerodynamic. It can have either a V6 or V8 engine. Each version has a top speed of about 130 miles per hour (209 km/h).

Here is a GL450. The GL line of SUVs were chosen as Motor Trend's SUV of the Year in 2007.

2013 GL550

Engine size	4.6 liters
Number of cylinders	8
Transmission	Automatic
Gearbox	7 speeds
0–60 mph (0–97 km/h)	5.5 seconds
Top speed	130 mph (209 km/h)

S-Class

The modern-day S-Classes originated with the six-cylinder Ponton W180 and W128 models that were made in 1954. Since then, the S-Class has become much more refined in its design and more powerful in its performance. S-Class sedans are among the more expensive Mercedes-Benz models, starting at $93,000. These luxurious sedans are stylish, elegant, and of the highest quality.

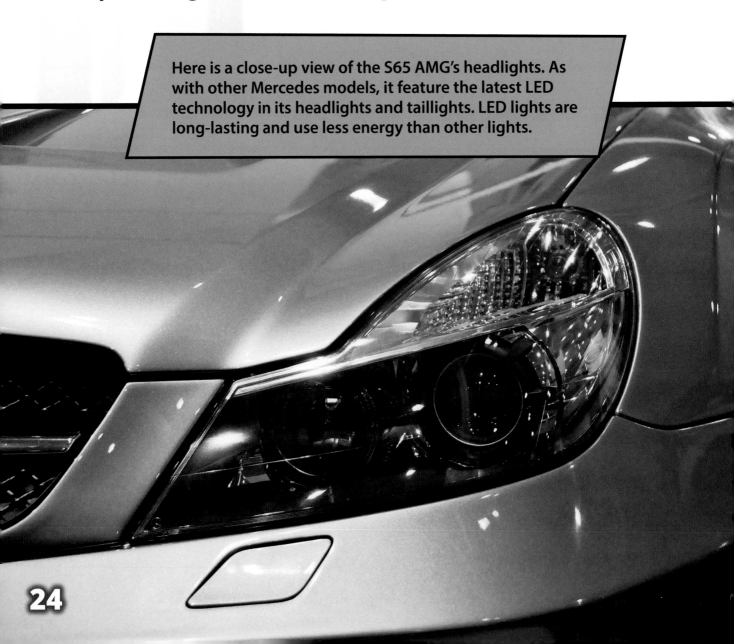

Here is a close-up view of the S65 AMG's headlights. As with other Mercedes models, it feature the latest LED technology in its headlights and taillights. LED lights are long-lasting and use less energy than other lights.

Here is an S400 HYBRID sedan.

2013 S65 AMG

Engine size	6 liters
Number of cylinders	12
Transmission	Automatic
Gearbox	5 speeds
0–60 mph (0–97 km/h)	4.2 seconds
Top speed	186 mph (300 km/h)

Mercedes-Benz currently has six different models within the S-Class. They are the S350 BlueTEC, the S400 HYBRID, the S550, the S600, the S63 AMG, and the top-of-the-line S65 AMG. The S65 AMG is also the most powerful of the S-Class models. The S65 AMG has a V12 engine. V12 engines are large and powerful. They are not very common and are used only in very expensive sports cars. The S65 AMG has a top speed of 186 miles per hour (300 km/h). It is fast and sporty, but, like all Mercedes-Benz models, it also has an interior designed for luxury and comfort.

SLS-Class AMG

The SLS-Class was first introduced in 1954. The models of the SLS-Class are extremely fast and sporty. They are meant to be sports cars that feel more like racecars than Mercedes' other cars. In 2012, Mercedes introduced the SLS AMG GT. There are two versions, a hardtop and a convertible.

This SLS AMG GT is showing off its gullwing doors.

2013 SLS AMG GT

Engine size	6.3 liters
Number of cylinders	8
Transmission	Automatic
Gearbox	7 speeds
0–60 mph (0–97 km/h)	3.6 seconds
Top speed	197 mph (317 km/h)

The SLS AMG, shown here, is a very expensive model. Its starting price is more than $200,000!

The SLS AMG GT is a two-seater with two doors. The doors on the SLS AMG GT are not like other doors, though. Instead of opening out to the side, like most cars, the doors open upward. They are called gullwing doors because when they are open they look like the wings of a seagull. The SLS AMG GT has a very short back and a long nose. Under the hood is a V8 engine. It has a top speed of 197 miles per hour (317 km/h).

Mercedes Moving Forward

As Mercedes-Benz moves into the future, it must keep up to date. The company has started making hybrid vehicles, which get better gas mileage and are better for the environment. It also introduced a line of compact cars in late 2013. They are called the CLA-Class. The CLA-Class is based on the A-Class, which is not available in the United States. These compact sedans will give Mercedes-Benz lovers yet another stylish, high-quality option.

Mercedes-Benz has a legendary history and played an important role in the development of automobiles. The company has an even brighter future. Mercedes-Benz's commitment to engineering and innovation made it successful in the past and continues to make it successful to this day.

Mercedes unveiled the CLA-Class as a concept car at auto shows in 2012. The first production year for this class is 2014.

Comparing Mercedes

CAR	YEARS MADE	TRANSMISSION	TOP SPEED	FACT
Ponton	1953–1962	4–speed manual	78 mph (125 km/h)	Almost 600,000 were produced.
W114 & W115	1968–1976	4–speed manual	99 mph (159 km/h)	Nearly 2 million W114s and W115s were sold.
E–Class	2007–	7–speed automatic	155 mph (249 km/h)	E–Classes are often used as taxis in Europe.
GL–Class	2010–	7–speed automatic	130 mph (209 km/h)	Most GL–Class models are assembled in Alabama.
S–Class	1954–	5–speed automatic	186 mph (300 km/h)	In German, the S–Class is the S–Klasse, which is short for *sonderklasse*. That means "special class."
SLS–Class	2011–	7–speed automatic	197 mph (317 km/h)	Mercedes–Benz is planning to introduce an electric SLS in 2013, called the SLS AMG Electric Drive.

Glossary

aerodynamic (er-oh-dy-NA-mik) Made to move through the air easily.

chassis (CHA-see) The part that holds up the body of a car.

commissioned (kuh-MIH-shund) Asked someone to do a job.

competitors (kum-PET-ih-torz) People or companies who are making and selling similar goods.

economy (ih-KAH-nuh-mee) The way in which a country or a business oversees its supplies and power sources.

engineering (en-juh-NEER-ing) The planning and building of engines, machines, roads, and bridges.

exclusive (eks-KLOO-siv) Not available to everyone.

hybrids (HY-bruds) Cars that have an engine that runs on gasoline and a motor that runs on electricity.

innovators (ih-nuh-VAY-terz) People who develop new goods or ideas.

luxurious (lug-ZHOOR-ee-us) Very comfortable and beautiful.

patented (PA-tent-id) Being granted a document that stops people from copying an invention.

pollutants (puh-LOO-tantz) Man-made waste that harms Earth's air, land, or water.

sedans (sih-DANZ) Cars that seat four or more people.

World War I (WURLD WOR WUN) The war fought between the Allies and the Central Powers from 1914 to 1918.

World War II (WURLD WOR TOO) The war fought by the United States, Great Britain, France, China, and the Soviet Union against Germany, Japan, and Italy from 1939 to 1945.

Index

Websites

Due to the changing nature of Internet links, PowerKids Press has developed an online list of websites related to the subject of this book. This site is updated regularly. Please use this link to access the list: www.powerkidslinks.com/smach/merce/